To Caorin

from L

GW01035778

# SILKIE

Retold by
## Liz Gough

Artwork by
## Rita Duffy

## Preface

The first discovery for me of a Silkie tale was in my school reader. I loved the story, it floated my imagination away from the mundane desk out through the classroom window, swimming far out to sea. Swimming and reading are two great passions in my life and the drawings in this little book confirms the third.

Rita Duffy

## About Silkie

A mythological, aquatic creature which has shape-shifting abilities, the Silkie appears in seal form. With the casting of sealskin by moonlight a human shape emerges, so very beautiful to behold it takes the breath away.

Quiet bays and lonely stretches of shore line allow the Silkie race to dance and sing in celebration of their mortal shape. Stories abound in Irish, Scottish, Icelandic and Faroese folklore. Many are woven around the need to satisfy human longing and desires. Whether it's a yearned for child, or a desire for love, traditional tales tell of the stealing or hiding of the abandoned seal pelt. Trapped on land as dawn rises the captured creature can only return to the sea again if the sealskin is returned to, or found by it's rightful owner...

and therein lies a tale to tell.

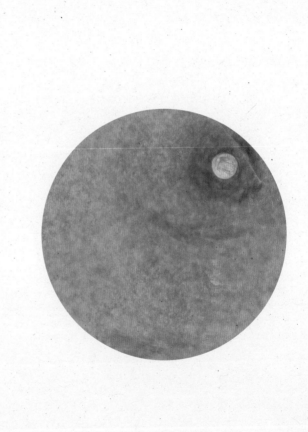

Once there was a fisherman who lived in a fine well furnished cottage not ten minutes walk from the bay in which he fished. He owned a small rowing boat, a curragh, which he had made with his own hands and strong woven nets which he mended in the light of day after a night's fishing. He told himself that he fished at night because the catch was better then. The fish could not see him in the darkness, which indeed was true. But deep inside he knew the real reason. He fished at night because he could not sleep. Tossing and turning, his heart lay heavy in his chest with the weight of loneliness. A cold empty bed at the end of the day was not a welcome resting place for a man who yearned for a wife and children.

Morning time was fine. He would lean on the side
of the upturned boat mending nets and sorting fish,
friends and passers-by stopping to chat. He enjoyed
company, calling at the market on the way home
to sell his catch and eat a hearty breakfast with the
market traders. After he would return home to sleep
for a few hours, rising in the late afternoon. The
rest of day passed quickly as he kept himself busy
around his home which he took great pride in.

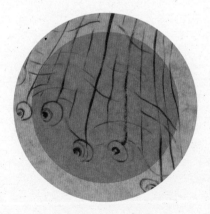

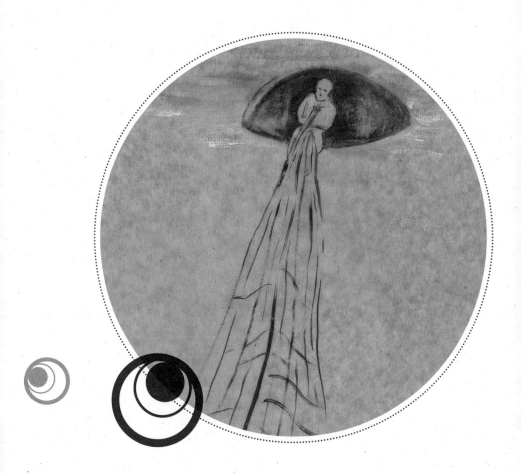

A sensible hard-working man he had invested his money in land, building a solid stone cottage and furnishing it well. White delph dishes and cups sat neatly on shelves and gleamed in the glow of the fire, constant warmth in the blackened grate. Dark oak furniture stood on the red tiled floor surrounded by whitewashed walls. Clean and tidy by nature he enjoyed keeping it that way.

## "I AM A LUCKY MAN TO OWN SUCH A FINE PLACE INDEED,"

he reminded himself one bright night as he closed the door behind him. The moon accompanied him along the way lighting the narrow beach path which curled through the dunes. Down in the bay the fisherman pushed his vessel seaward. Soon the air was filled with the sound of oars as the boat cut through a silver ribbon of moon-light streaming across the water.

# "IT'S TOO BRIGHT FOR A GOOD CATCH TONIGHT,"

he told himself as he cast the nets over then settled down in the boat waiting for what fish there might be in the calm waters below.

It was long before dawn when the fisherman rowed easily back to shore, his nets holding what few fish he had caught. He would finish early. Such a small catch would take no time at all to pack for market.

Dragging the curragh on to firm sand he turned the vessel upside down to dry and laid the oars at it's side. The fish were easily sorted and the fisherman lay back against the curve of the boat. The lapping sound of waves soothed him as he rested and he pulled his thick moleskin jacket around him snugly for warmth. Soon he was dropping off to sleep in the peace of the night.

'SPLISH SPLASH SPLISH SPLASH'

# 'SPLISH SPLASH SPLISH SPLASH'

## HE WOKE FROM HIS SLUMBER.
## "WHAT WAS THAT?"

There it was again, he wasn't imagining it at all. The fisherman quietly raised himself up and looked over the top of the upturned boat to see where the noise was coming from. Not twenty feet away three seals were swimming to shore. One by one they left the water and lay basking on the sand. Their skins shone blue-black in the moonlight, dark eyes mirrored small moons in each. The fisherman smiled to himself.

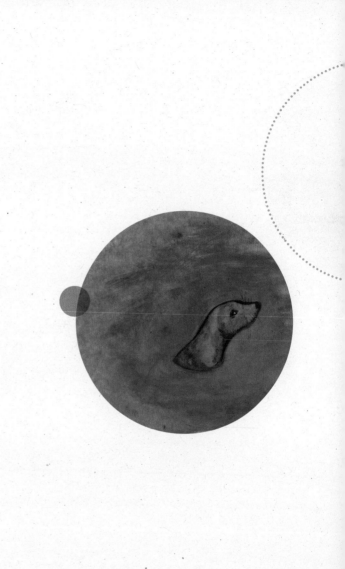

**H**ow lucky he was to see such beautiful creatures just yards away from him. He had spotted seals before bobbing in the distant water or basking on protruding rocks, but never so near. The seal closest to him moved suddenly away from her sisters and looking all around ran up the beach as if to check there was no one watching.

He held himself very still crouching behind the boat, breathing as quietly as he could. He did not want to be discovered or frighten the creatures away. Then the strangest thing happened. Nodding to the other two seals as she returned, they all stood up together on their back flippers. Front flippers raised they pulled away their seal fur which tumbled down forming blue-black silky mounds on the sand. No longer seals, three beautiful women with long, wavy blue-black hair, glistening skin and eyes that mirrored small moons in each stepped free.

The sound of laughter accompanied them as they ran skipping and dancing along the shore. Rubbing his eyes the fisherman looked again at the scene before him. What was he watching?

He had heard stories of seal people, seal women more beautiful than words could describe. He never believed them to be true, until now.

After what seemed like minutes the women returned to their skins. The fisherman watched as the first pulled the blue-black pelt back over her body, the second followed suit, their seal forms returning instantly. They waited patiently in shallow water as the youngest woman reluctantly followed, calling on her to hurry before the dawn came. Slowly pulling her mantle of fur over her body, she took a last wistful look at glistening skin before it disappeared. The fisherman was sure he heard her sigh. She entered the water behind the others and they swam away just as the redness of the rising sun warmed the horizon.

He walked back through the dunes that morning in a daze not waiting to speak with his friends or stay for breakfast with the market traders. The hunger for food and company had left him. All he could hear in his head was her sigh, all he could see in his thoughts was the wistfulness in her eyes and the whiteness of her skin. All he could feel in his heart was the desire to know her name. He knew something had happened within him. This surely was love, he had found love. He was in love with the youngest seal woman.

For weeks he dreamt of nothing but her. Each night as he rowed out into the bay his heart raced, fit to burst in his chest with longing for her; but to no avail. The fisherman returned home at dawn disappointed. His friends and neighbours worried about him for a while. He had grown silent of late and had lost weight, he just wasn't himself at all. Weeks grew into months and the fisherman's love survived only in his dreams, fading in the reasoned light of day. His mind was playing tricks, loneliness had allowed his imagination to run away with him, that was it.

## "I AM A SENSIBLE MAN,"

he told himself.

## "I MUST HAVE BEEN DREAMING AFTER ALL. SURELY SUCH BEAUTIFUL CREATURES COULD ONLY LIVE IN STORIES OR DREAMS."

Winter passed, spring had blossomed into summer when finally the fisherman settled back into his daily routine. Slowly he started to come round to himself again. When taking breakfast with the market traders or passing time with friends, he never mentioned what had happened that night for fear they would laugh at him and his vivid imagination.

It was late in August when a full moon rose over the bay, shining with such intensity it seemed as if day had not yet passed. It was only the silver coldness of the light that betrayed night's presence. A sprinkling of early stars hinted in the sky as the fisherman made his way easily through the knee-high dune grasses and down to the beach. Fishing had been good for weeks and he carried freshly woven nets across the shoulders of the fine new jacket he was wearing, bought that morning at market. Before leaving the house he had admired himself in the mirror. The jacket sat well on him. He had chosen this one in particular for the practical deepness of the pockets and the feel of it's rich, dark green lining.

On reaching the shore line he turned the curragh right-side up and pushed the little vessel out into deeper waters. The sound of oars cutting cleanly through calm sea accompanied him as he rowed effortlessly out into the middle of the bay. The next few hours passed slowly. As the fishing was poor the fisherman returned to shore long before dawn with sparsely filled nets. What little fish there were he sorted for market in no time at all then settled against the upturned boat and closed his eyes, enjoying the warmth of the summer's night. After weeks of heavy backbreaking work and long hours the fisherman was grateful for the rest and he drifted off easily to sleep and to dream.

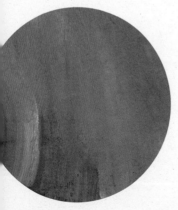

A wonderful smile appeared on the fisherman's face as he slept. He was dreaming of her swimming to shore. He could hear her laughter as she cast her sealskin on golden sands and stepping from it ran up and down the beach with her sisters.

This time she ran further and further away from them, so far that they called out loudly to come back. The sound of their voices so real it seemed as if he wasn't dreaming at all. The fisherman woke with a start, the calling continued to ring in his ears. He rubbed his eyes in an attempt to wipe sleep away and slowly looked over the top of the upturned boat. There in front of him not twenty feet away were two seal women stepping into blue-black pelts that lay on the golden sands at their feet. They were calling anxiously for their sister to return.

Far, far down the beach a tiny figure waved and turned back towards them. Reassured, her seal sisters entered the water and swam out into the bay.

It was then the fisherman did what he shouldn't have done. Mesmerised, as if still in a dream, he found himself flat on his belly throwing a fishing line out to catch the edge of the last blue-black pelt. Once hooked he pulled it towards him. Sliding back behind the curragh, he then rolled it up, burying it deep in the inside pocket of his jacket next to his now pounding heart.

It was then he heard a sound nearby and looking up over the boat he saw the youngest seal woman. Distraught, sighing and crying she was running up and down the water's edge calling to her sisters, but to no avail. They had disappeared as they must do, just before the redness of dawn warmed the horizon.

The realisation that her sisters were truly gone frightened her. She sank to her knees covering her skin with long, silky blue-black hair and crying quietly to herself in distress. It was then she heard the voice of a man speaking to her. She had only seen and heard such creatures on boats while she swam in the bay or basked with her sisters on protruding rocks.

Looking up with eyes that mirrored small moons in each she saw a tall man looking back at her. He spoke kindly, asking her why she was crying and holding out a coat that was the colour of the dark green sea she knew so well.

"I HAVE LOST SOMETHING THAT IS VERY
PRECIOUS TO ME SIR. IT'S MY MANTLE
TO KEEP ME WARM. IT'S MADE OF SILKY
FUR AND BLUE-BLACK IN COLOUR.
HAVE YOU SEEN IT?"

He bent over and wrapped his coat around her.

# "HERE IS MY COAT TO COVER YOU. IT WILL KEEP YOU WARM. COME BACK TO MY HOME AND WE WILL LOOK AGAIN LATER."

He held out his hand and helped her to her feet. The seal woman did not know why she took his hand. All she knew was that her heart skipped a beat when he had spoken to her.

She was standing beside him now. Looking up she studied his face framed by waves of fiery red curls which tumbled over grey eyes. He was looking back with such longing any fear she had left her immediately. She nodded and keeping her hand in his walked back through the sand dunes to the comfort of his home.

She never returned to look for her sealskin for it was there she fell in love with the world of Man. She saw fire burning in the grate and felt it's warmth. The white shiny dishes, wooden furniture and linens delighted her as she made her way around the cottage touching everything in sight. He cooked for her that evening. Such smells and tastes in this new and wonderful land filled her with the desire to stay, and in the staying led her to forget.

In a very short time she found herself falling in love with the fisherman, his world and all that it had to offer.

They married soon after, and as the years passed the house filled with children. A bigger house was needed and so the fisherman set about building a fine house fit for a wife and growing family. He asked his wife to start clearing out and packing as they would move before winter set in.

She set about her tasks soon after and was handed a dusty parcel by her eldest daughter, reached down from the highest shelf at the back of a cupboard.

"IS THIS FOR PACKING MOTHER OR FOR THE BIN?" SHE ENQUIRED.

"I DON'T KNOW WHAT'S IN IT DARLING. LEAVE IT OVER BESIDE THE BOOKS ON THE CHAIR BY THE FIRE. I'LL LOOK AT IT LATER."

It was well after everyone's bedtime when she remembered the parcel and unsorted books.

Quietly so as not to disturb him sleeping in bed beside her, she made her way downstairs and over to the bundle on the chair by the fire. Lying next to the books a brown paper parcel sat covered in dust. One by one she placed the books on the floor in front of her, sorting as she went along, those for keeping, those for giving away. She lifted the parcel last. Chair cleared she sat down and stared at the tightly knotted string. The parcel was not hers, she had no recollection of it at all. Anyway she would not tie string that tightly as it was a devil to unfasten. As she sat by the glow of the fire patiently untying the knot a shiver rang down her spine. She wasn't cold but never the less something was making the hairs on her body lift and her skin tingle.

## THE BROWN PAPER WAS DRY AND UNFORGIVING. IT CRACKLED AS SHE UNFOLDED EACH CREASED PANEL UNTIL THE CONTENTS LAY IN FULL VIEW ON HER KNEE.

A smooth, blue-black pelt lay neatly folded. She ran her hand across the fur and felt it's sleekness. The touching made it roll forward and she watched as it tumbled down forming a blue-black silky mound at her feet. She slid from the chair and buried her face in it's folds.

A knowing began to flow through her. Water lapping over rocks. Sea birds circling above. The softness of sand beneath her belly. Swimming at speed through shoals of fish. Wave after wave of remembering quickly came crashing in round her. She heard the sound of her seal sisters calling out to her. She could see their eyes mirroring small moons in each as their heads bobbed above water in the bay. She could taste the sea in her mouth.

The sky was covered with a thick blanket of storm clouds. No moon or stars to light the way as she stumbled down the path through the dunes and onto the beach. The wind was blowing from the sea sending froth-whipped waves smashing along the shore line. Lifting her face to the elements she smelt a storm brewing out beyond the headland. It would not be long before it hit the bay.

There was no time to waste. Quickly she unfastened her hair then stepped out of her night clothes. Skin tingling in the cutting wind she unfolded the blue-black pelt and pulled it around her. Taking one last look at her white skinned limbs she stretched it over her head and returning to the water's edge heard her sister's cries. Far out in the bay two seals waited as a lone seal made it's way through choppy waters to meet them. Diving down below the swirling currents they swam swiftly away together to calmer waters. The storm hit the bay just before dawn.

Next morning the fisherman woke early. Wind and rain beating against the windows offered no peace and little chance of sleep. He turned to find the bed empty, his wife must be up already. He dressed quickly and made his way downstairs for breakfast. How strange, the kitchen was quiet, no food cooking and table bare his wife was nowhere to be seen. He turned for warmth to the fire which lay dying in the grate. Neat piles of books stood in a row in front of the vacant chair. It was then he saw something on the floor at his feet.

It was an opened parcel. The sight of one sheet of creased brown paper and untied string stopped his heart and took the breath from him. His legs left him and as he staggered to the chair and sat, instant tears washed his face. He wiped them away and searched frantically around the floor in front of him. Nothing. It's contents and his wife were missing.

The knowing was with him now. Out into the storm he ran pushing against buffeting winds and lashing rain, down through the sand dunes and onto the beach. He was sure he heard seal's calling as he squinted through the squall out into the bay. Salt water and sand-laden wind stung his face as he struggled to push the curragh out to sea, storm high waves refusing him entry to deeper waters. Yet he tried and tried again until he collapsed exhausted on the shore.

It was later that afternoon when the storm had passed
the fisherman returned. A flat expanse of calm sea
stretched as far as the eye could see with barely
a ripple making it to shore; he scanned the bay in
search of her. The curragh took easily to the water
now and he rowed quickly out to the edge of the bay
calling to her as he went. Many hours passed before
finally he gave up. She was nowhere to be seen and
the fisherman rowed back to shore alone.

She was gone.

H e returned home that night to their children who waited anxiously for news of their mother. Gathering his sons and daughters around him in the kitchen he told the story as each child listened intently. He spoke of the first night he saw her and had fallen in love with her. What he had done to keep her; he had stolen her sealskin and hidden it so frightened he was that she would leave. She had fallen in love with him too and his world and never asked for it nor looked for it since. Then it had been discovered again after many years.

"In the finding your mother must have returned to her kind," he explained. "The calling was too strong, for she is of the seal people. She is Silkie.

## THAT IS WHY YOUR HAIR SHINES BLUE-BLACK THE COLOUR OF SEAL FUR, YOU HAVE WEBBED SKIN BETWEEN YOUR FINGERS AND TOES AND YOUR EYES CHANGE LIKE THE COLOUR OF THE SEA."

It is said from that day onwards the fisherman never had to work again for each night as he slept minding their children a lone seal made her way to the shore. Time and time again she returned with mouthfuls of fish until a fine catch lay not twenty feet from the little boat. Exactly on the spot where they had first met.

# The Storyteller
# Liz Gough

Liz Gough lives and works in Belfast where she was born. The early sixties and seventies contrasted greatly in the city, providing two very differing worlds for the childhood and adolescent years that Liz would experience while growing up in West Belfast.

Educated in St. Dominic's Grammar School Falls Road, Liz returned to education as a mature student and mother of two sons. She received her B.ED in Drama and English at St. Mary's College, Queen's University Belfast in 1989. Having completed her teaching degree, Liz has continued to work in education throughout her career.

Immersed in oral tradition tales and literature in her formative years, she has taken her childhood passion for stories into her adult life. Much of her work has featured on both TV and radio. A member of Storytellers of Ireland, Liz has performed in many differing venues both at home and around the world.

Building on the commissions she has received and most recent award in recognition of her work, Liz has established 'talestotell' to promote and celebrate the role stories have in our everyday lives, history and identity.

## The Artist
## Rita Duffy

Rita Duffy was born in 1959 in Belfast. She received her BA at the Art and Design Centre and her MA in Fine Art at the University of Ulster. She is one of Northern Ireland's ground breaking artists who began her work concentrating primarily on the figurative/narrative tradition. Her art is often autobiographical, including themes and images of Irish identity, history and politics. Duffy's work has grown and evolved but remains intensely personal with overtones of the surreal. Homage is paid to the language of magic realism and always there is exquisite crafting of materials.

She has initiated several major collaborative art projects and was made an Honorary Member of the RSUA for her developmental work within the built environment.

Her work is increasingly shown in solo and group exhibitions around the world. She is an associate at Goldsmiths College, London working on an artistic exchange between Argentina and N.Ireland. Her Belfast studio practice continues to develop and her public art projects are increasingly preoccupied with international themes.

Currently she holds a Leverhulme Fellowship with the Transitional Justice Institute, looking at the role visual art has in post conflict societies.

Duffy's work is being increasingly collected at home and abroad with work in numerous important public and private collections. To date she has achieved a long list of awards, "medals" and bursaries for her public and privately commissioned work.

# Thanks

Thanks to Ciaran Hurson and Christopher Martin at Hurson for their design, Chris Hill photographer and UnLtd The Foundation for Social Entrepreneurs.